GOD'S FAMILY

The Greatest Royal Family Ever

Catherine Mackenzie

Illustrated by Tessa Janes

Imagine you could be a prince or a princess for a day?

What things would you need?

A Crown? A Carriage?

A Castle?

What things would you do?

Make laws? Wave nicely?

Wear expensive clothes?

Where would you go?

Foreign countries? Rich homes?

Fancy parties?

But can you really be a princess? Is it possible to be a prince? Is your dad a king? Is your granny a queen? Do people bow and curtsy to you when you walk down the street? Probably not.

But did you know that God is the King of everything? If you trust in him he is your Heavenly Father.

God is everything the perfect dad should be – but better.

Trusting in God makes you a child of God and part of the greatest royal family ever.

Do you love Jesus? Have you trusted in him to save you from your sins? Do you know what that means? If not, then God wants you to find out.

To be part of the greatest royal family ever you don't need crowns or carriages but you will need some special lessons…

For God is the King of all the earth; sing praises with a psalm! Psalm 47:7

Royal Lesson No. 1

God wants to show you what you are like. You need to see the bad things you've done. These are called sins. Sin is when you say, do or think things that God doesn't like. Sin is when you don't say, do or think the things that God loves.

You need to know that you are a sinner so that you can know God saves sinners.

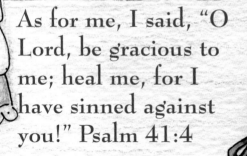

As for me, I said, "O Lord, be gracious to me; heal me, for I have sinned against you!" Psalm 41:4

Royal Lesson No. 2

God wants to show you what he is like. He wants you to know that he is strong and mighty. God is just, fair and perfect in all things – wonderful in every way. All of God is lovely – lovelier than the loveliest jewels, more beautiful than the most precious gold.

God is so lovely he loves us even when we are unlovely.

Let them give thanks to the Lord for his unfailing love and his wonderful deeds for mankind.
Psalm 107:31 (NIV)

Royal Lesson No. 3

God wants you to know that he hates sin, but loves to save sinners. God loves sinners so much he wants to free them from sin and from the punishment of sin. So Jesus lived a sinless life and took the punishment for sin when he died on the cross. He was punished instead of sinners and sinners who trust in Jesus get all the good things they don't deserve … like God's forgiveness, Jesus' righteousness and eternal life.

For our sake he made him to be sin who knew no sin, so that in him we might become the righteousness of God. 2 Corinthians 5:21

God loves sinners so much he wants to free them from death. So when God raised Jesus back to life, death was defeated. Eternal life is given to all those who turn from their sin to trust in God. And eternal life is a life that is sinless, perfect, full of joy and that lasts forever.

Whoever believes in the Son has eternal life; whoever does not obey the Son shall not see life, but the wrath of God remains on him. John 3:36

The richest royal family in the world could never be as happy as God's family is.

Royal Lesson No. 4

God wants you to know that he loves sinners so much that he has yet another gift for them. This gift is faith. We can't make it or find it. Only God can give it to us. When God gives us faith, he gives it to us so we can trust and believe in him. God loves sinners so much that he gives them everything they need to be his child. You can't buy God's gifts, you can't earn them, you can only say 'Yes, please!'

All God's gifts are free of charge.

God does not give faith to everyone. Not every sinner is saved and becomes God's child. Only those who believe in God and in his Son, Jesus Christ, receive eternal life.

It is because of his love and goodness that he gives this gift to anyone. God is good, holy, loving and fair.

For the wages of sin is death, but the free gift of God is eternal life in Christ Jesus our Lord. Romans 6:23

Royal Lesson No. 5

God's children must love God and trust him. They must trust God the Father – who gave his Son. They must trust God the Son – who gave his life. They must trust God the Holy Spirit – who comforts God's people and helps them to obey God, to love him and to believe.

God's children must obey him. But doing good things doesn't get God's children to heaven. Our good works are never good enough for that – Jesus is the only one good enough. He did everything that was needed to give sinners everlasting life when he lived a perfect life, died on the cross and rose from the dead. Our good works don't make God love us any more than he does already.

His love is always 100%. But our good works do show others a little bit of what God is really like. And good works are good for us. God gives us these good works to do.

Another wonderful gift from our Heavenly Father.

For we are his workmanship, created in Christ Jesus for good works, which God prepared beforehand, that we should walk in them. Ephesians 2:10

Royal Lesson No. 6

God's princes and princesses should live lives that give honour to their Heavenly Father. They should be kind and gentle, patient and loving, joyful, peaceful, faithful and self-controlled. They should not lose their tempers. They shouldn't sulk, or answer back or pick a fight. But they do. God's children still struggle with sin. God works in the lives of his children so that over time they become more like Jesus—even though they still disobey God. However, because God is at work in their lives God's children hate sin, and repent of it.

They want to run away from sin and run to God instead.

God knows that his people have to fight against sin and he gives them his strength to do this. Whenever God's people feel that they want to sin, the strength that God has given them is all they need to say no to sin and yes to God.

But now that you have been set free from sin and have become slaves of God, the fruit you get leads to sanctification and its end, eternal life. Romans 6:22

Royal Lesson No. 7

So if royal princesses go to parties and princes travel to foreign lands, where do God's children go?

God's children will go anywhere that God tells them to go, so that they can tell others about God and his wonderful gifts, especially the gift of his lovely Son, Jesus. God's children want to tell others about how faithful, peaceful, gentle and patient God is. They want to sing and shout and give God all the glory.

God's children will tell the world about God's amazing love.

My mouth is filled with your praise
and with your glory all the day. Psalm 71:8

Royal Lesson No. 8

Some of God's children will go to other countries, others will stay at home. All of them have important work to do for God, their Heavenly Father. They must go to poor and rich, boys and girls, old and young to tell them that everyone needs to be saved from sin.

They long to tell others that there is only one who can save us from sin –

Jesus Christ.

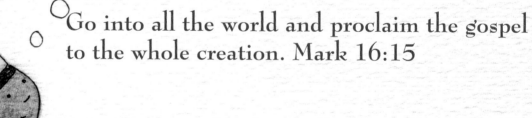

Go into all the world and proclaim the gospel to the whole creation. Mark 16:15

8

Royal Lesson No. 9

All God's children will one day go to heaven to be with him. There will come a time in everyone's life when they will stop living.

Those who trust in Jesus will immediately go to heaven.

Heaven is a glorious place with no sin, sickness or sadness. The part of God's child that goes straight to heaven is called the soul. The soul is the part of you that loves God or that doesn't. It is the part of you that wants to obey God or that doesn't. But what happens to the bodies of God's children? They will stay behind on earth until the day God says it's time to come back to life.

9

And God raised the Lord and will also raise us up by his power.
1 Corinthians 6:14

Royal Lesson No. 10

Then the bodies of God's children will be raised from the dead to an eternal life free of sin, sickness and sadness. Every one of God's children, every member of God's royal family, will be with him forever in the New Heavens and the New Earth. The eternal life of the believer will be perfectly beautiful in every way. Eternity with our Heavenly Father God will be the best and greatest celebration ever. Nothing will be wrong there. Everything will be right.

10

One day the bodies of God's people will be there too.

They will be free of sin, pain and sadness and full of joy, strength, beauty, goodness, love and peace. So many good things will be theirs forever.

The dead will be raised imperishable, and we shall be changed. 1 Corinthians 15:52

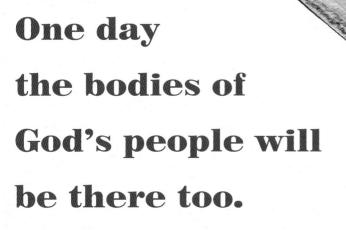

God's princes and princesses, every one of his forgiven and saved children, will be forever with their King of kings.

Jesus our Saviour.
Jesus our Lord.

And this is the testimony, that God gave us eternal life, and this life is in his Son. 1 John 5:11

What about you? Have you learned these royal lessons? Has this truth made it from your head to your heart? Do you trust in Jesus Christ to save you from your sin? There's no one else you can go to for salvation, forgiveness and eternal life!

And this is eternal life – to know the only true God and Jesus Christ whom he sent.

God's Family, will capture your children's imaginations, educate their minds and reach their souls. Unlike many children's books, that water down the gospel, Catherine Mackenzie's book presents a clear and solid gospel message, creatively woven through ten royal lessons that every budding prince or princess will want to learn. Complimented by Tessa Janes' heart-warming illustrations–every family should pick up a copy of this book.

MARTY MACHOWSKI – *Pastor and author of The Gospel Story Bible, Long Story Short, and Old Story New.*

In ten lessons that will connect with young princes and princesses everywhere, Catherine Mackenzie explores the royal treasure that is being in the greatest royal family. I love the way she highlights God's grace, a life of repentance, and the Christian's missionary identity. I also love how Tessa Janes' beautiful illustrations highlight the diversity–age, race, gender, and ability–we find within God's kingdom people.

JARED KENNEDY–*Pastor of Families, Sojourn Community Church*

Absolutely love it! It is simple but thorough in helping children of all ages understand what it means to become a Christian.

CONNIE DEVER–*Wife of Mark Dever, Senior Pastor, Capitol Hill Baptist Church, Washington D.C.*

Your children are never too small and never too young to begin to learn who they are and whom they need. Treat them like royalty by reading them this little book which will introduce them to the family of God.

TIM CHALLIES–*Blogger at www.challies.com*

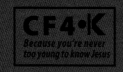 

Christian Focus Publications publishes books for adults and children under its four main imprints: Christian Focus, Christian Heritage, CF4K and Mentor. Our books reflect that God's Word is reliable and Jesus is the way to know him, and live for ever with him.

Our children's publication list includes a Sunday school curriculum that covers pre-school to early teens; puzzle and activity books. We also publish personal and family devotional titles, biographies and inspirational stories that children will love.

If you are looking for quality Bible teaching for children then we have an excellent range of Bible story and age specific theological books. From pre-school to teenage fiction, we have it covered!

Find us at our web page: www.christianfocus.com

10 9 8 7 6 5 4 3 2 1

© Copyright 2014 Catherine Mackenzie

ISBN: 978-1-78191-356-7

Published by Christian Focus Publications, Geanies House, Fearn, Tain, Ross-shire, IV20 1TW, U.K.

Cover design: Daniel van Straaten

Illustrations by Tessa Janes

Printed in China

All Scripture quotations, unless otherwise indicated, are from The Holy Bible, English Standard Version, copyright © 2001 by Crossway Bibles, a division of Good News Publishers. Used by permission. All rights reserved. ESV Text Edition: 2007.

Scripture quotations marked (NIV) are taken from the HOLY BIBLE, NEW INTERNATIONAL VERSION®. NIV®. Copyright©1973, 1978, 1984 by International Bible Society. Used by permission of Zondervan. All rights reserved

All rights reserved. No part of this publication may be reproduced, stored in a retrieval system, or transmitted, in any form, by any means, electronic, mechanical, photocopying, recording or otherwise without the prior permission of the publisher or a licence permitting restricted copying. In the U.K. such licences are issued by the Copyright Licensing Agency, Saffron House, 6-10 Kirby Street, London,   EC1 8TS. www.cla.co.uk

RED FOX
DOES WHAT?
SURELY NOT!

CHRISTINE CHAMBERS

Christine
2023
xx
xx

JELLY BEAN BOOKS 2023

Red Fox loves his friends Arctic Fox and Silver Fox. They are coming over today for a special tea party. He hasn't seen them for a long time. Red Fox loves to bake. He is making a scrummy cake to share.

Red Fox sets the timer and pops the cake mix in the oven, then clears the table to set up for tea. He finds his favourite table cloth, with the bright flower print; and his finest china, with the curvy cup handles. He loves to make a fuss!

The timer goes **PING!**

Excitedly, he opens the oven door. Red Fox frowns – what's gone wrong?

Oh no! Red Fox does what? *Surely not!*

He realises that he's the missed the eggs out of the recipe!

He does, he does!

The cake is like stodgy porridge. He will have to start again.

Red Fox mixes the ingredients, checking carefully that everything is correct this time.

Yes, he is sure that it is right. He sets the timer once again and puts the cake mix in the oven.

Red Fox washes up the dishes from the first cake. He is happy. This time there is no mistake.

The timer goes **PING!**

Confident, Red Fox opens the oven door. The cake smells delicious and looks perfect. With his oven gloves on, he carefully takes it out. He turns to the table and...

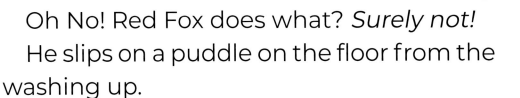

Oh No! Red Fox does what? *Surely not!*

He slips on a puddle on the floor from the washing up.

"He does! He does!"

The cake flies through the air and crashes down, exploding everywhere – up the walls and on the floor.

Red Fox feels sad. He will have to start all over again!

Red Fox mixes more ingredients and everything looks in order. He puts the cake mix in the oven for the third time, feeling rather pleased with himself.

But time is running out!

His friends are due to arrive soon. He has just enough time to bake *this* cake.

Red Fox sets the timer.

After cleaning and drying the floor, he makes a cup of tea and puts his feet up.

He closes his eyes and falls fast asleep.

The timer goes **PING!**

Red Fox does not move. He is dreaming that he is dancing on marshmallow clouds, and fizzy jelly disco lights are sparkling in the sky.

The cake continues to cook. It gets hotter and hotter. Blacker and blacker.

Oh No!

Red Fox does what? Surely not!

He burns the cake.

He does, he does!

With a jump, Red Fox wakes up. The kitchen is full of smoke, with a burning smell in the air. Red Fox takes out the cake. There is no way it can be saved. He throws it in the bin and opens the windows. Fox cries.

There's not enough time to start again! he thinks. *Any moment now my friends will arrive. They will see the cake on the walls and smell the smoke. Worst of all, there is no cake to share.*

Red Fox is so upset. Today was supposed to be so special.

He decides to pretend not be at home, and hides in the corner behind the bin.

The doorbell rings, but Red Fox does not move. His friends shout out to him, but he stays quiet. As they look through the open window, they notice the mess, smell the smoke, and spot Red Fox hiding in the shadows.

"Red Fox, we see you!" they call. "Open the door. We will help you clean up." Red Fox does not move. "Don't worry, we're here to help."

Red Fox slowly gets to his feet and opens the door. His friends give him a big squishy hug.

"It's all right, Red Fox," they say. "Let's clear up together and start again."

With everyone helping, it doesn't take too long.

Once again the timer goes **PING!**

This time it is perfect.

Placing the cake on the table, Red Fox says, "You are my best friends. I love you both!"

His friends smile.

Red Fox feels so much better.

Then they all tuck into a large piece of warm spongy chocolate cake. Somehow it tastes even better with the friendship and love that went into baking it. They all agree that it's the most delicious cake they have ever tasted.

Red Fox's cheeks start to glow a little pinker. His smile stretches a little wider.

And for that moment, Red Fox feels like the luckiest fox in the world.

He does, he does!

Colour in this picture...